Life Story of a
Salamander

Charlotte Guillain

Heinemann
LIBRARY

Chicago, Illinois

© 2016 Heinemann Library
an imprint of Capstone Global Library, LLC
Chicago, Illinois

Edited by Catherine Veitch and Gina Kammer
Designed by Richard Parker and Peggie Carley
Picture research by Mica Brancic
Production by Steve Walker
Originated by Capstone Global Library Ltd

Library of Congress Cataloging-in-Publication Data
Cataloging-in-publication information is on file
with the Library of Congress.

ISBN 978-1-4846-0490-8 (hardcover)
ISBN 978-1-4846-0495-3 (paperback)
ISBN 978-1-4846-0505-9 (eBook PDF)

Acknowledgments
We would like to thank the following for permission to
reproduce photographs:

Alamy: Rolf Nussbaumer Photography, 9; Dreamstime: Kcmatt,
24; FLPA: Imagebroker/Reinhard Hölzl, 5, Minden Pictures/
Do Van Dijck, 4, Minden Pictures/Sebastian Kennerknecht, 16;
Getty Images: John Cancalosi, cover, 21; iStock: Snowleopard1,
8, 28 (left); Nature Picture Library: Barry Mansell, 14; Science
Source: E. R. Degginger, 7, 10, 11, 28 (right), FLPA/Dave
Pressland, 13, Gary Meszaros, 12, 29 (left), Joseph T. Collins,
17, 18, Stephen Dalton, 26, Tom McHugh, 19; Shutterstock:
AlexussK (stone design element), cover and throughout,
EcoPrint, 6, jannoon028 (grass border), throughout, Jason
Mintzer, 25, Matt Jeppson, 29 (right), reptiles4all, 27, Yuliya
Proskurina (green leaves border), cover and throughout;
SuperStock: Biosphoto, 15, 23, F1 Online/F. Rauschenbach, 20,
imagebroker, 22

We would like to thank Michael Bright for his assistance in the
preparation of this book.

Contents

Some words are shown in bold, **like this.** You can find out what they mean by looking in the glossary.

What is a Salamander?

A salamander is a type of animal called an **amphibian.** Amphibians are animals with backbones that can live in water and on land. All amphibians have soft, damp skin.

Salamanders look a bit like lizards, but they have no scales on their skin. Salamanders live in most parts of the world and can be large or small. They have four legs and a long tail.

A Salamander's Life Story

Like all other animals, a salamander goes through different stages as it grows into an adult. These stages make up the animal's life story.

adult

young

Follow the life story of salamanders, and watch them change in unusual ways as they develop and grow.

It Starts with an Egg

A salamander starts its life as an egg. The egg is **transparent,** with a dark dot in the middle.

Spotted salamanders lay eggs in water. The eggs are covered with a jellylike coating. Other salamanders keep eggs in their bodies.

The Egg Hatches

The mother leaves eggs in a pond or stream. A **larva** grows inside the egg until it is ready to hatch.

When the larva hatches, it swims away. A salamander larva can only live in water.

The Larva Changes

A salamander larva has feathery **gills** that let it breathe underwater. Its long tail helps it swim.

A salamander larva eats tiny animals in the water. It grows and changes. This change of body shape is called **metamorphosis.**

Changing into an Adult

Finally, the salamander larva grows front legs and lungs, so it can breathe on land. The adult salamander can live on land and in water.

Some salamanders grow to be nearly 6 feet (1.8 meters) long. Other salamanders grow to be 6 to 10 inches (15 to 25 centimeters) long.

An adult salamander spends most of its time on land. It lives in dark, damp places close to water. Its skin needs to stay moist and cool.

Some salamanders escape from **predators** by letting their tails drop off. While the predator watches the wriggling tail, the salamander can escape!

Some **species** of salamander spend more time in water and don't have any back legs. Other salamanders have four legs to move around on land.

Some salamanders can use their tails to help them climb trees. Other salamanders' tails help them balance as they move.

Salamander Food

A salamander eats insects, worms, and slugs. It flicks out its sticky tongue to catch **prey**. A salamander sees its prey in the daytime and smells its prey at night.

prey

A salamander has small, sharp teeth to grip prey when it is caught. Muscles in the salamander's throat push the food down so it can swallow.

Mating

A salamander looks for a mate so they can continue the life story. Together they can **reproduce** and create new salamanders.

Salamanders mate on land. It usually happens at night during the summer. Some male salamanders become more colorful when they are looking for a mate.

The male salamander finds a female and rubs her with his chin to show he is ready to mate.

After mating, some female salamanders keep the eggs in their bodies until the **larvae** hatch. Other salamanders lay their eggs in water and leave them there.

A Salamander's Life

Salamanders **hibernate** during the cold winter months. They hide under rotting logs or rocks. They come out again in spring when the weather is warmer.

Salamanders may be killed by diseases or **predators,** such as snakes or birds. Some adult salamanders can live for more than 20 years in the wild.

Salamander Life Story Diagram

egg

young larva

adult salamander

older larva

Glossary

amphibian animal that can live on land and in water

gills body parts that animals use to breathe under water

hibernate spend the winter resting or sleeping

larva stage in an animal's life before it becomes an adult; more than one larva are larvae

metamorphosis stages where an animal changes body shape and appearance

predator animal that hunts and eats other animals

reproduce to lay eggs or give birth to young

species name for a type of living thing

transparent see-through

Find Out More

Books

Chinese Giant Salamander: The World's Biggest Amphibian, Ann O. Squire (Bearport Publishing, 2007)

Deadly Factbook 3: Reptiles and Amphibians, Steve Backshall (Orion Childrens, 2013)

Salamanders, Molly Kolpin (Capstone Press, 2010)

Websites

http://www.bbc.co.uk/nature/life/Salamander
Visit the BBC Nature website to find out more about salamanders and watch video clips.

http://kids.nationalgeographic.com/kids/animals/creaturefeature/
Click on "amphibians" on the National Geographic website and find out about spotted salamanders.

Index